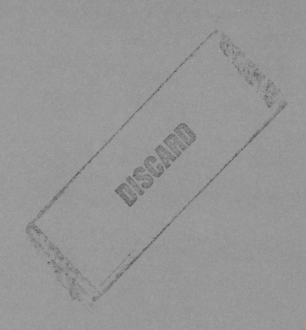

PLANT FAMILIES

Carol Lerner

Morrow Junior Books
New York

For Caroline Rubin, with affection

The author thanks William J. Hess, Curator of the Herbarium at the Morton Arboretum, Lisle, Illinois, for reviewing the manuscript.

Printed in Hong Kong.
3   4   5   6   7   8   9   10   11   12
Library of Congress Cataloging in Publication Data
Lerner, Carol.
Plant families.
Summary: Provides simplified descriptions of twelve of
the largest families of flowering plants in North
America.
1. Plants—Identification—Juvenile literature.
2. Botany—Classification—Juvenile literature.
[1. Plants—Identification.   2. Botany]   I. Title.
QK97.5.L47   1989   582.13'097   88-26653
ISBN 0-688-07881-8
ISBN 0-688-07882-6 (lib. bdg.)

Contents

Introduction

The world's plants show an endless variety of colors, sizes, and shapes. New plants are still being discovered, and botanists think that the total number of different species is over a third of a million.

In spite of all their differences, many species of plants do resemble other ones. From the earliest times, people have tried to put them into some kind of order by placing plants that are alike in some important ways in groups.

One of the earliest ideas was to organize them according to their size and their general appearance. All of the trees were put in one group, bushes in another, and so on. But as people learned of more and more plants, they needed better ways to order the growing number.

Over the centuries many different systems were tried and then discarded, but sometimes a part of a rejected system was carried over into the new ones. One idea that has been used ever since the seventeenth century is to divide all flowering plants into two groups according to the number of their "seed leaves." People knew that every time a seed sprouts, the young plant has either one or two seed leaves or cotyledons (cot-i-LEE-duns) that supply food to the seedling until it grows real leaves.

The plants within each of these two large groups share other characteristics as well. The easiest ones to see are in the leaves and flowers. Plants with one seed leaf usually have leaf veins running in rows down the length of the leaf, like railroad tracks. Their petals and other flower parts are usually in threes (three, six, nine, and so on). The last four families in this book have single seed leaves, but you will see some exceptions to the general rule. Plants with two seed leaves usually have veins arranged like a net over the leaf, and flower parts that come in fours and fives.

In the eighteenth century, the great botanist Linnaeus (Lin-NAY-us) invented a new system for ordering plants that paid special attention to the *stamens,* the male parts of a flower. Plants were put into different classes according to the number of stamens, their length, and whether the stamens grow separately or are joined to one another.

Plant scientists were not satisfied with this system for very long. They saw that many plants with similar stamens are different in every other way and don't really belong together. They wanted a "natural system" that would put together the species that are actually related to one another. But unlike the members of human families, plants have no birth certificates. The only evidence of a close relationship comes from the plants themselves. These botanists looked at every part of a plant—not just one or two parts—to discover overall similarities between different species. Today we have a great deal of new information that those botanists did not have, but we still use their groups to bring order into the plant world.

Species that have a great deal in common are put together into the same *genus*. The genus may contain a great many species but sometimes it holds just one. Different *genera* (the plural of genus) that appear to be closely related are then grouped together in a plant *family*.

While clues about family membership may be found in any part of the plant, often the best information comes from the flowers. A flower has just four main parts. On the underside there is a ring of *sepals*, usually green. The *petals* are just inside the sepals. In the center of the petals are the male parts that make the pollen, the *stamens*. *Pistils*, the female parts, are in the middle of the stamens. Often a plant lacks one or more of these flower parts. For example, many plants have flowers with stamens but no pistils, because the male parts grow on some of their plants and the female parts on others.

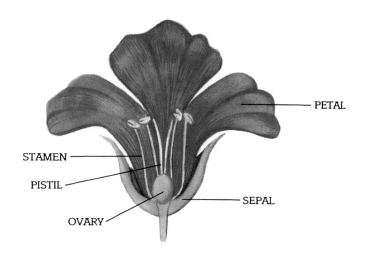

The stamen and the pistil are the flower parts that make seeds. To do this, a grain of *pollen* from a stamen must first reach the tip of a pistil. Soon afterward, the wall of the tiny grain of pollen breaks open and male cells that were inside it move down to the bottom part of the pistil, called the *ovary*. When a male cell joins with an egg cell inside the ovary, a seed begins to grow.

When you examine a living plant to learn about it and its family, choose one with a flower that is fully open. Count the number of sepals, petals, and other parts; look at their shape; and see how the parts are attached to each other. If it is a plant that you can pick, it may be easier to see all of the parts and how they are connected by taking the flower apart, starting with the sepals on the outside. If you are using a garden plant, the number of flower parts may differ from plants that grow in the wild. Most garden roses, for example, have far more petals than the five on a wild species.

Of course, by picking the flower, you destroy its ability to make seeds. Plants that are rare or plants that grow in protected places—on nature trails or in forest preserves, for example—should not be picked. The majority of the plant examples shown in this book are common wild flowers or weeds that grow on vacant lots and by roadsides. Usually the family description includes the names of several other plants that can also be used for study.

If some of the plants have finished blooming, you may be able to find some of their fruits. Speaking in the language of botany, a *fruit* is the plant's ripe ovary with its seeds. Therefore, a peach and a strawberry are fruits, and so are an acorn, a green bean, and a grain of wheat. In this book, the word *fruit* is used with this meaning.

When trying to identify a plant, notice its other parts, too. See whether the stem is round or whether it is flattened on some sides. Look at the shape of the leaves and how they are arranged on the stem. Watch for other clues, as well: Some plants have a strong odor that you can smell when you crush a leaf, and some have hollow stems.

Botanists have named about three hundred families of flowering plants. Although this book describes only twelve of them, these twelve families contain hundreds of wild flowers and weeds growing in all parts of North America. They include the world's largest plant families—those with the greatest number of different species.

The descriptions given for these twelve families are simplified ones. Since their purpose—and that of this book—is to give quick clues to family membership, they focus on plant parts that can be seen most easily and are most helpful for identification. The position of pistils and the internal arrangements of their ovaries—essential to a complete botanical description—are largely ignored here.

The twelve plants used as examples in the illustrations appear in life size. Details are drawn in enlargements; most of these details are big enough on the plant so they can be seen without a magnifier. A small, inexpensive hand lens that enlarges ten to twenty times is helpful in looking at the smallest of them.

Some special botanical words, which are used in this introduction and in the family descriptions, are shown in *italics* at first mention. They are defined in the glossary at the end of the book. The name of the plant shown in each illustration appears in SMALL CAPITAL LETTERS in the text.

Buttercup Family

RANUNCULACEAE
(ra-nun-kew-LAY-see-ee)

This family contains about 1,500 different species and almost 300 of these are native plants of the United States and Canada. The Latin name, *Ranunculaceae,* means "little frogs" and hints at where buttercups grow. Many of the most common plants in the family are at home in wet or marshy places.

The buttercup family is also known as the crowfoot family because many species have leaves like those on the CREEPING BUTTERCUP: Each leaf is divided into several parts, with deep cuts between the sections—similar to a bird's footprint. The leaf stems are often wide at the bottom and wrap around the stem of the plant.

The most common flower arrangement for plants in this family is five sepals and five petals, but the pattern is often different. Different species have three to fifteen sepals and there may be as many as twenty-three petals—or none at all. Flowers with no petals often have colorful sepals that look like petals. Marsh marigold, with bright yellow sepals, is an example.

The center of the flower gives the best clues to buttercup family membership. Most often, flowers have many pistils (sometimes hundreds) and many stamens (twenty to fifty). The pistils are arranged in circles on a cone-shaped structure and surrounded by rings of stamens. After being fertilized, this kind of flower forms a cluster of small dry fruits.

Some species break away from this simple pattern. Columbine has petals that extend backward into long thin tubes, called "spurs." Monkshood also has petals with spurs, and larkspur has a spurred sepal.

Some plants in the family also have fruits that are different from the fruit of creeping buttercup. Columbine, larkspur, and monkshood make a dry *pod,* and the fruit of baneberry is a *berry.*

Many of our best-known wild flowers belong to the family, including anemone and rue anemone, hepatica, meadow rue, and dozens of different kinds of buttercups. Creeping buttercup is not a native plant but a weed from Europe that has now spread across North America. Clematis and peony, as well as all the spurred flowers in the family, are popular garden plants.

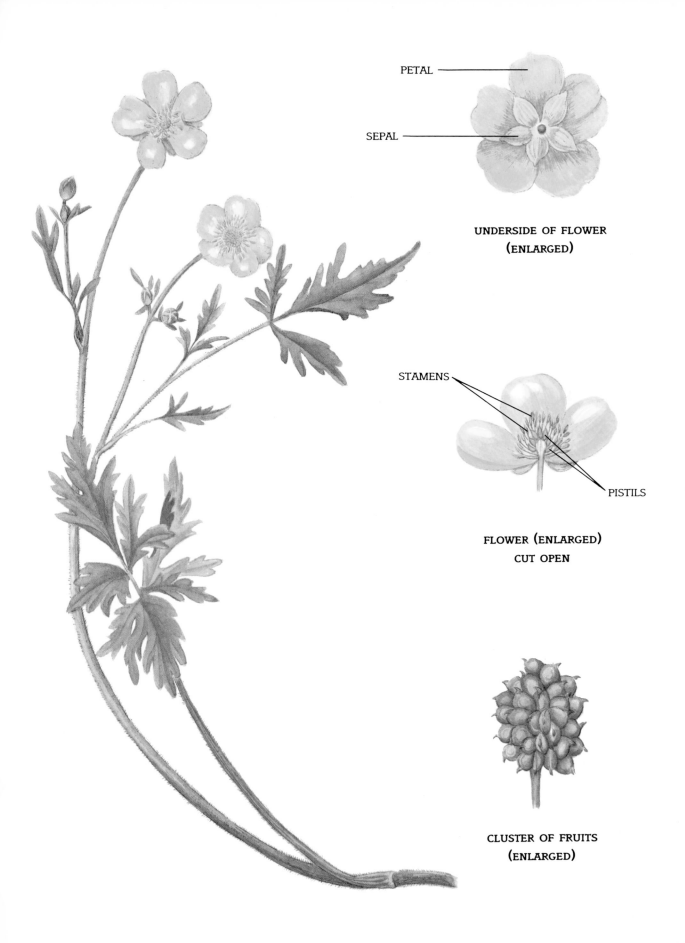

PETAL

SEPAL

UNDERSIDE OF FLOWER
(ENLARGED)

STAMENS

PISTILS

FLOWER (ENLARGED)
CUT OPEN

CLUSTER OF FRUITS
(ENLARGED)

Mustard Family

CRUCIFERAE
(crew-SIF-fer-ree)

This big family has about 2,500 species, with large numbers in the United States and Canada. It is easy to identify a member of this family by its flowers. They always grow in clusters and the four petals of each flower are arranged in the shape of a cross. The Latin name, *Cruciferae,* means "cross-bearers." Six stamens grow around the center of the cross. The two in the outer ring are shorter than the four in the inner circle. The petals are surrounded by four sepals, and a single pistil stands in the middle. The stems of mustard plants contain a watery juice. This sap often has a strong smell.

The typical mustard fruit is a unique kind of *pod.* When this fruit is ripe, its two outer walls break open at the bottom and reveal a thin wall in the center of the pod. The seeds are attached to this wall. The pods are either long and narrow or short and rounded, as on the common weed called "shepherd's purse." A few mustards have fruits that do not split open.

Many vegetable foods are mustard plants: cabbage, cauliflower, broccoli, brussels sprouts, turnip, and radish, among others. Mustard seed and horse-radish root come from the family. It also contains a large number of garden flowers, including stocks, candytuft, and alyssum. Some attractive wild flowers belong to the family, such as toothwort and the wallflowers of the West, but mustards are much more familiar growing as weeds. YELLOW ROCKET (or winter cress) is found in most parts of the United States and Canada. Spring pastures are often filled with these bright golden flowers. Peppergrass and garlic mustard are two other weedy mustards that are widespread.

PETAL

FLOWER (ENLARGED)

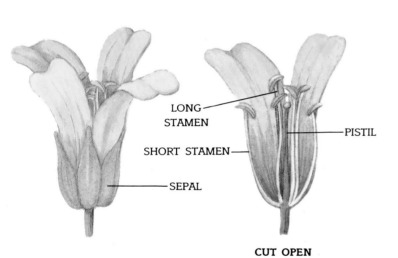

LONG
STAMEN

PISTIL

SHORT STAMEN

SEPAL

CUT OPEN

FLOWER (ENLARGED)

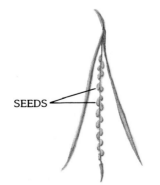

SEEDS

FRUIT (ENLARGED)

Pink Family

CARYOPHYLLACEAE
(car-ee-o-fi-LAY-see-ee)

This is a numerous family in North America and one that grows in most parts of the continent. You can often identify family members by looking at their stems. Most have *simple* leaves (that is, leaves with the blade or flat part all in one piece) that grow in opposite pairs up the plant stem. The stem itself is usually swollen at the points where the leaves grow. The pairs of leaves are often joined at the bottom: Sometimes they are connected by a line or ridge around the stem; in other species, the lower parts of the two paired leaves have grown together and they circle the stem.

Flowers in the pink family have sepals that are joined—at least at the bottom—and petals that are separate from one another. There are usually five of each, but sometimes four. The tips of the petals often have a notch in the middle. There are up to ten stamens, and the tip of the pistil may split into two to five *styles*.

The fruit of most pinks is a *capsule,* a kind of dry fruit that breaks open when it is ripe. Capsules in this family usually hold many small seeds and split open at the top.

BOUNCING BET was brought to America from Europe and now is common along roadsides, railroad tracks, and in other sunny areas. It is also called "soapwort" ("soap plant"). In colonial times, people crushed its leaves and mixed them with water to make a soap.

Campions, catchflies, and corn cockle are other wild flowers in the family. It also contains many florist and garden flowers: carnations, baby's breath, sweet William, and—of course—pinks. The most common family members of all are the weedy chickweeds that invade lawns and gardens.

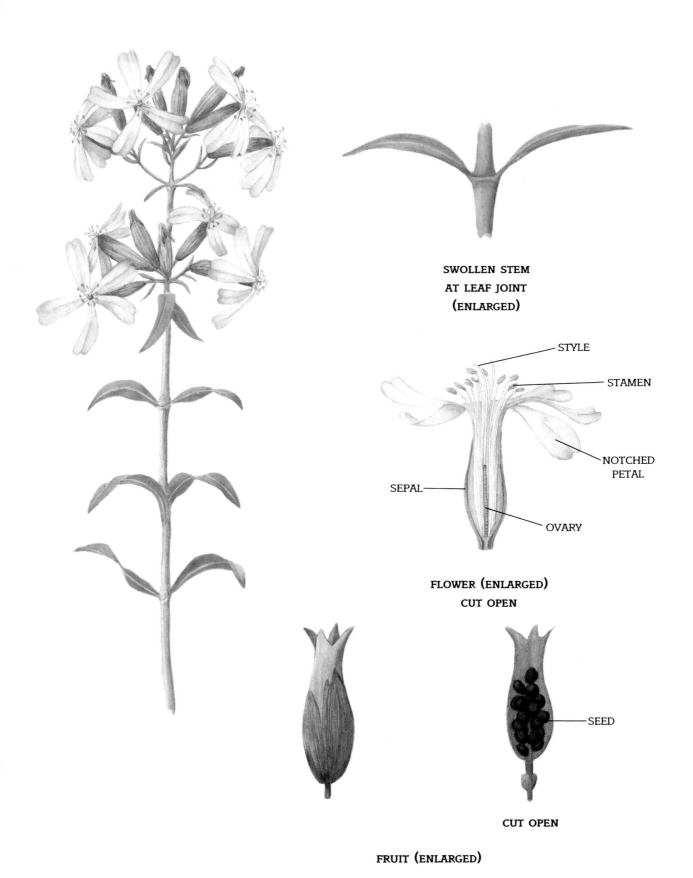

SWOLLEN STEM
AT LEAF JOINT
(ENLARGED)

STYLE

STAMEN

NOTCHED
PETAL

SEPAL

OVARY

FLOWER (ENLARGED)
CUT OPEN

SEED

CUT OPEN

FRUIT (ENLARGED)

Mint Family

LABIATAE
(lay-bee-AY-tee)

The mints are one of the most common plant families in North America and are usually easy to recognize. The family's Latin name, *Labiatae,* comes from the word for "lip" and describes the flowers: Their five petals are joined together at the bottom to form a tube, but the tube splits into two parts at the top of the flower. The two upper petals form an upper "lip," while the three lower ones are the lower "lip." The flowers are usually small, but there are many, growing in clusters. On some mint plants, the clusters are mainly at the ends of the stems. On others, they grow in the angles where the leaves attach to the stem and make a little wreath of flowers around the stem.

The flowers most often have four stamens, but some kinds of mints have just two. There is one pistil, forked at the tip. The fruit of a single flower is four little *nutlets.*

Mints have a square stem: You can feel this by rolling it between your fingers. Leaves grow in pairs opposite each other along the stem.

Like many other mints, CATNIP has a strong smell. The odor comes from oil produced in many small glands all over the surface of its leaves and stems. Some cats find the smell delightful, but other kinds of mints are more pleasing to people. Leaves of basil, thyme, marjoram, sage, rosemary, oregano, and peppermint are all used to flavor our foods. The oil of lavender is used in making perfume.

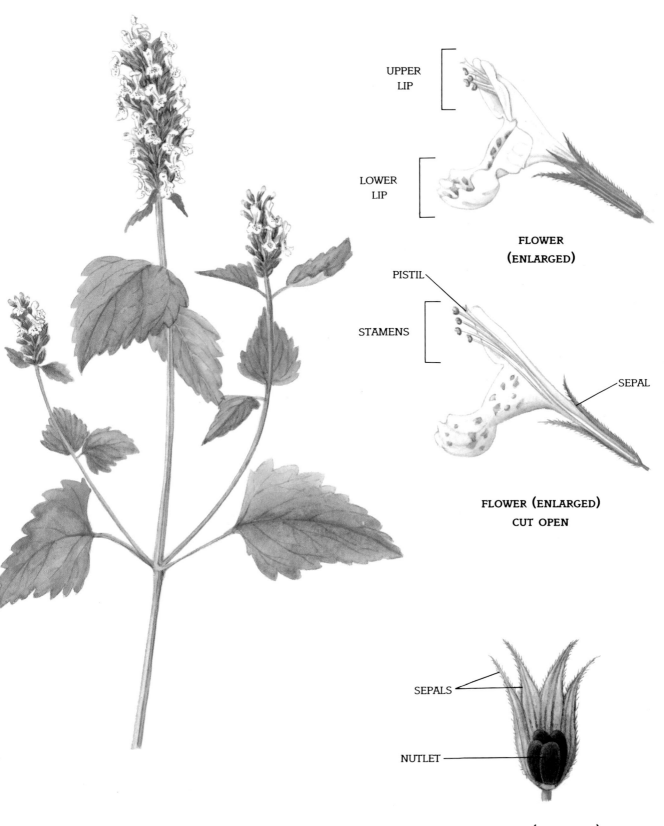

UPPER
LIP

LOWER
LIP

**FLOWER
(ENLARGED)**

PISTIL

STAMENS

SEPAL

**FLOWER (ENLARGED)
CUT OPEN**

SEPALS

NUTLET

**FRUIT (ENLARGED)
WITH ONE SEPAL
REMOVED FROM PLANT**

Pea Family

LEGUMINOSAE
(le-gyu-men-NO-see)

This is one of the very largest plant families in the world, with about 13,000 different species. The Latin name, *Leguminosae,* comes from the typical fruit of the family, a *legume* (LEG-yume). The legume is a *pod,* such as a pea pod or a green bean, with two or more seeds inside. When it dries, the legume breaks open along the two long edges of the pod and splits into halves. Not all fruits in the family split open: Some break apart at the joints between each seed, and others do not open at all.

Most members of the pea family growing in the United States and Canada are easy to recognize by their unusual flowers. They have five sepals, but these may be hard to count because they are more or less joined together. The five petals have different shapes and some of them are joined, too; the two lower ones are attached except at their tips. Two more petals—called the "wings"—surround them. The fifth petal is on top. The stamens and a single pistil are tucked inside the two lower petals.

BLUE LUPINE, one of the dozens of wild lupines in North America, shows the arrangement of the stamens. The ten stamens are joined to form a tube. In some other family members, one of the stamens grows separately from the other nine.

Not all of the 13,000 species have the same kind of flower. Those on the mesquite plant of the Southwest, for example, have a ring of five tiny petals around a cluster of stamens that are twice as long as the petals. This flower looks nothing like the typical pea flower of the lupine.

Because of such differences, some botanists disagree about putting all of these plants together into a single family. Instead, they separate them into three different families. But in spite of differences in the flowers, the fact that their fruits are similar is evidence that all these plants are close relatives.

The pea family is an important source of food, containing all kinds of peas and beans, including peanuts. Soybeans and fodder plants, such as clover and alfalfa, feed livestock. Pea family wild flowers include many vetches, locoweeds, and lupines; and sweet peas and wisteria are garden flowers.

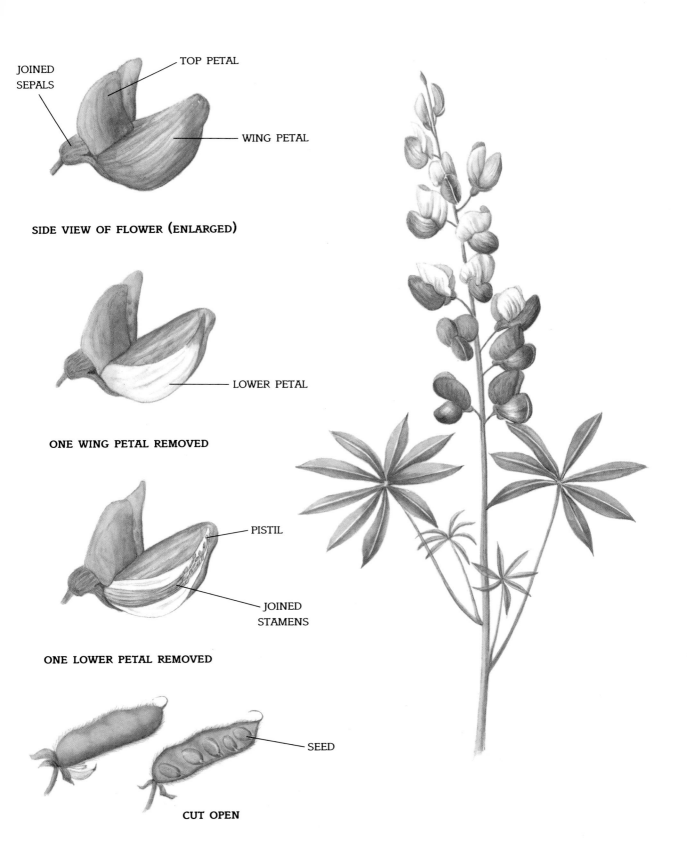

JOINED
SEPALS

TOP PETAL

WING PETAL

SIDE VIEW OF FLOWER (ENLARGED)

LOWER PETAL

ONE WING PETAL REMOVED

PISTIL

JOINED
STAMENS

ONE LOWER PETAL REMOVED

SEED

CUT OPEN

FRUIT

Rose Family

ROSACEAE
(row-ZAY-see-ee)

In many ways, the flowers in this large family (about 3,000 species) are alike. Most of the flower parts come in groups of five: five sepals, which may be joined together, and five petals. Usually there are many stamens, arranged in rings of five. There may be one pistil or many.

Most of the plants have a *floral cup* that grows beneath the flower. The cup may be a shallow saucer or a deep bowl or tube. Sepals, petals, and stamens are attached to the rim of this cup. Although it is quite easy to recognize a flower belonging to this family, their fruits come in many different forms. The great variety of the fruits comes in part from the shape of the floral cup and the way it grows after the flower is fertilized.

The PASTURE ROSE is one of the many species of wild roses in North America. Roses have a deep floral cup that encloses the many small *ovaries* of a rose flower. As the ovaries ripen into fruits, the floral cup grows, too. It becomes the red "rose hip" that contains the flower's small dry fruits.

The juicy part of an apple or a pear—both members of the rose family—is also the floral cup: The real fruit (the ripe ovary) of these plants is the seeds and other hard parts in the center that we throw away with the core. Other plants in the family have floral cups that remain small and do not grow around the fruits. Some of these fruits are big and juicy, such as plums and apricots, and others are small and hard. The fruit of a cinquefoil (SINK-foil) flower, for example, is a cluster of dry little fruits.

This family also contains raspberries, strawberries, cherries, and peaches. In addition to rosebushes, it includes many other trees and shrubs that are used to landscape gardens and parks, such as hawthorn, crab apple, shadbush, bridal wreath, and mountain ash.

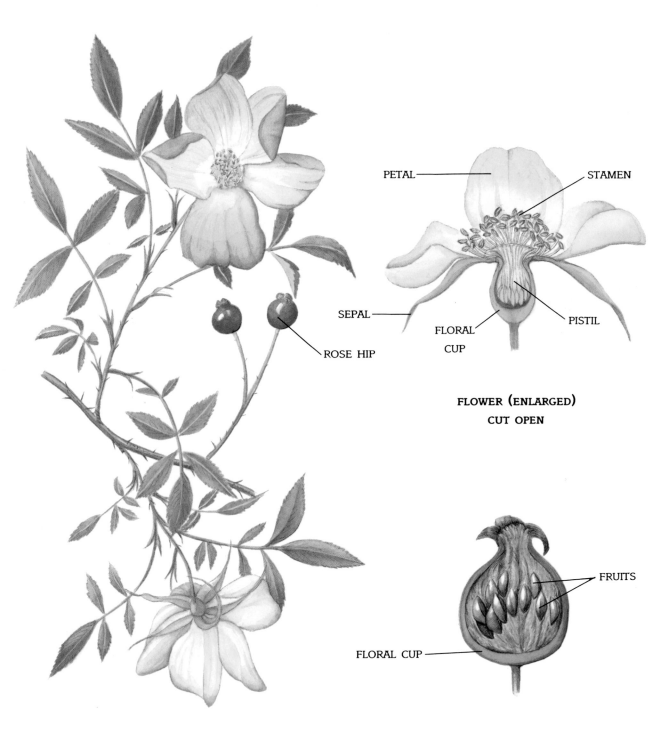

PETAL

STAMEN

SEPAL

FLORAL
CUP

PISTIL

ROSE HIP

**FLOWER (ENLARGED)
CUT OPEN**

FRUITS

FLORAL CUP

**ROSE HIP (ENLARGED)
CUT OPEN**

Parsley Family

UMBELLIFERAE
(um-beh-LIF-fer-ee)

This is a large family with about 2,500 different kinds of plants—350 in the United States and Canada alone. It gets its Latin name, *Umbelliferae,* from the way the flowers are usually arranged: Many small stalks curve upward from the top of a stem, like ribs of an umbrella turned inside out, and a small flower may bloom at the tip of each rib. The whole flat-topped cluster of these many little flowers is called an *umbel.* But usually, instead of a flower, there is another set of "umbrella ribs" growing at the top of these small stalks, and the little flowers grow at the tips of this second set of stalks. These smaller clusters are called "little umbels" or "umbellets."

Each tiny flower has five petals and five stamens. The *ovary* is out of sight, below the other flower parts. Each fertilized flower will produce a small hard fruit that splits into two identical parts after it dries.

Leaves of parsley family plants are usually divided into many separate parts or *leaflets.* The leaf stems are wide at the bottom and often wrap around the plant stem.

Many plants in the family have fragrant oils: Parsley leaves and the seeds from caraway, dill, anise, coriander, and cumin are used for flavoring. Celery stems and parsnip roots are eaten as vegetables. QUEEN ANNE'S LACE—the most familiar of all the umbel plants—is believed to be the wild ancestor of our carrots.

Since they often have a strong family resemblance and can be confusing, you should know that some umbel plants (poison hemlock and water hemlock, for example) contain strong poisons.

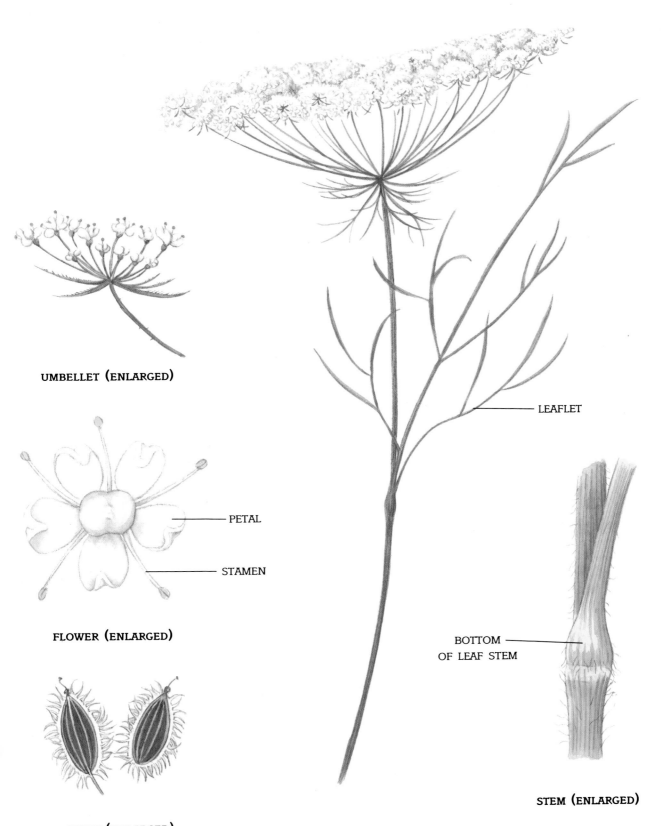

UMBELLET (ENLARGED)

FLOWER (ENLARGED)

PETAL

STAMEN

FRUIT (ENLARGED)

LEAFLET

BOTTOM
OF LEAF STEM

STEM (ENLARGED)

Composite Family

COMPOSITAE
(com-POZ-it-tee)

Botanists disagree about the number of composite species growing in the world: Recent estimates have been from 13,000 to 22,000! Whatever the correct number really is, we know that this is one of the largest of all the families of flowering plants.

What looks like a single flower on a composite is really a cluster of tiny flowers (called *florets*) growing close together on top of the same *receptacle*. The cluster may have just a few florets or over a hundred, and the florets are of two different kinds. Those in the center of many composites are arranged in a circle or disk. A *disk floret* has five tiny petals that join to form a tube around the stamens and pistil. Its five stamens are also joined into a tube. A single pistil sticks out above the tube of stamens. The top part of the pistil, called the *stigma,* splits into two branches at its tip.

A ring of *ray florets* surrounds the circle of disk florets. The five petals of a ray floret are joined at the bottom, but then the tube splits into a long flat tongue. Some composite flowers, such as thistles, have only disk florets; dandelions and some others have only ray florets.

The fruit of a composite floret is small and hard with one seed inside a tight, thin covering. Often the *pappus* of the floret stays attached to the fruit. When it does, the seeds have bristles (on thistle plants), little parachutes (on dandelions), or some other kind of hair or scales. These help to spread the seeds: Bristles hook on to the fur or clothing of a passerby, and the dandelion seed sails off on the smallest breeze.

ANNUAL SUNFLOWER is one of the many kinds of sunflowers that grow in North America. In this species, the ray florets have no stamen or pistil and do not make seeds.

Seeds from cultivated sunflowers are eaten and are pressed for their oil, but the most common food from the family is the leaves of lettuce plants. Asters, daisies, zinnias, and many other garden flowers are composites. Some of our most familiar weeds, such as chicory and ragweed, also belong to this family.

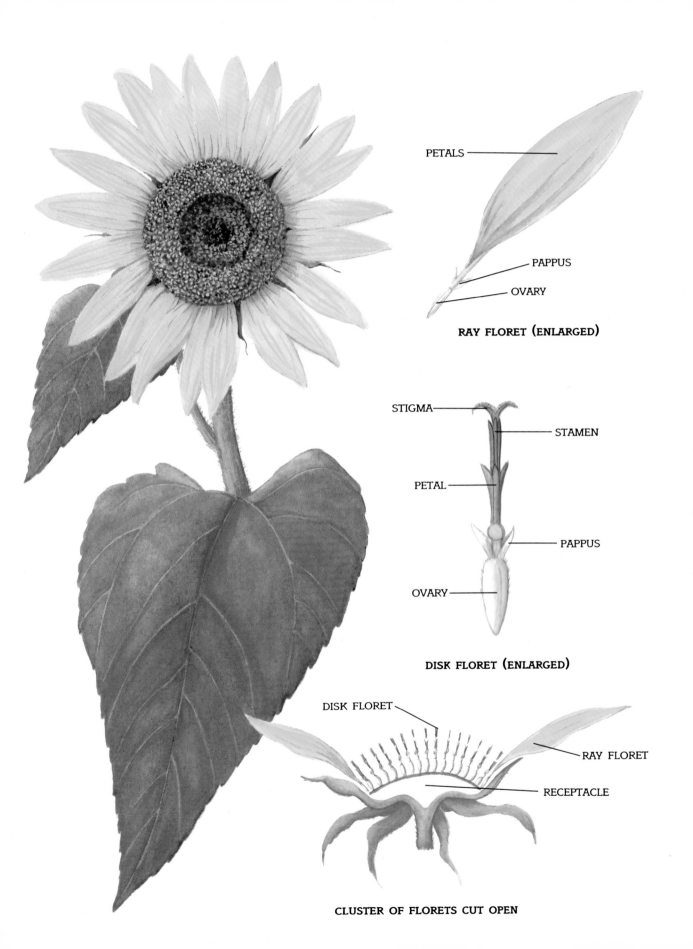

PETALS

PAPPUS

OVARY

RAY FLORET (ENLARGED)

STIGMA

STAMEN

PETAL

PAPPUS

OVARY

DISK FLORET (ENLARGED)

DISK FLORET

RAY FLORET

RECEPTACLE

CLUSTER OF FLORETS CUT OPEN

Lily Family

LILIACEAE
(lil-ee-AY-see-ee)

The lilies are a worldwide family with over 3,000 different species. Many are familiar plants in North America, both in gardens and in the wild.

The three sepals of a lily flower are often the same color as its three petals, so it looks as if the flower has six petals. If you take the flower apart, you see that these grow in two circles around the center: Three sepals grow in the outer ring and three petals in the inner one. Most plants in the family have six stamens. There is a single pistil.

The typical fruit is a *capsule* that splits open when it is ripe. Inside, the capsule usually has three sections, each with many seeds. Some lily plants, such as asparagus, have a *berry* as their fruit instead of a capsule.

Plants in the lily family have large underground parts that store up food. The thick rootstocks of daylilies and the bulbs of tulips are examples. We use the bulbs of onions and garlic to flavor our food.

LARGE-FLOWERED BELLWORT ("wort" is an old word meaning plant) is one of four yellow bellworts that flower in the spring woods of eastern North America. Other common wild flowers in the lily family are Solomon's seal, trout lily, trillium, Turk's-cap lily, sego lily, and the yuccas. The family also contains some of our best-known garden flowers, including hyacinth, lily of the valley, daylily, and star-of-Bethlehem.

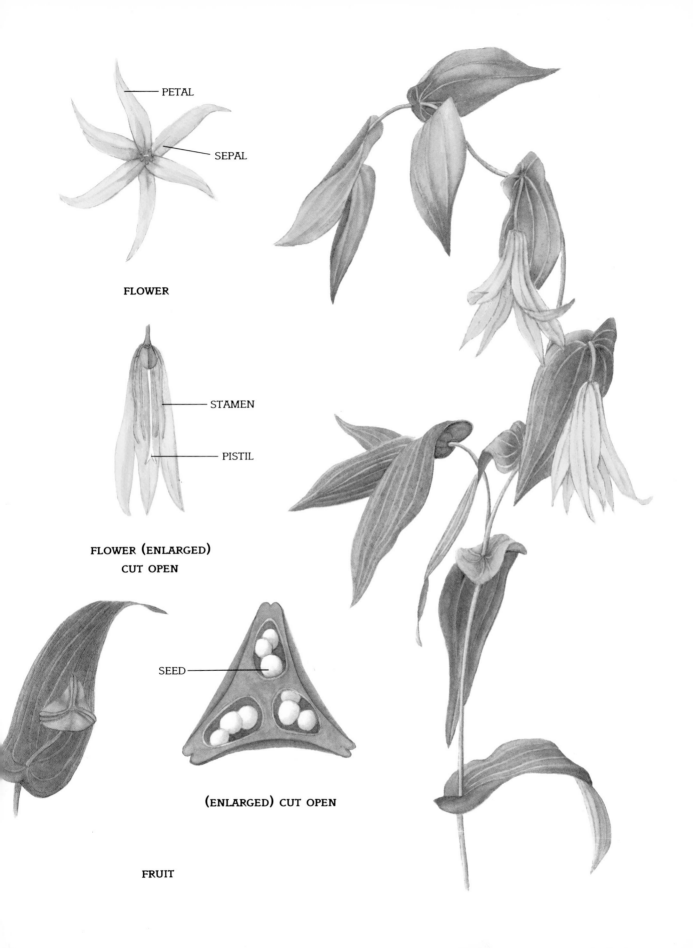

PETAL

SEPAL

FLOWER

STAMEN

PISTIL

FLOWER (ENLARGED)
CUT OPEN

SEED

(ENLARGED) CUT OPEN

FRUIT

Arum Family

ARACEAE
(air-RAY-see-ee)

This family can't be confused with any other. A thick spike, called the *spadix* (SPAY-dix), grows from the top of the stem. Tiny flowers are crammed together on this spadix. A leaflike flap, called the *spathe* (SPAYTH), is attached just below the spadix. Some species have spathes that are white or brightly colored, rather than green. The spathe often wraps around the spadix and surrounds the flowers.

The flowers are strange, too. They are tiny—often no larger than the head of a pin. Some species, such as skunk cabbage, have flowers with both stamens and pistils and a ring of four to six little scales that take the place of petals and sepals. Other arum plants have two kinds of flowers: some flowers with stamens only (male flowers) and others with a pistil only (female flowers). These have no ring of scales. Usually the fruit of an arum plant is a *berry*.

Arum plants that have separate male and female flowers usually carry both on the same spadix. JACK-IN-THE-PULPIT is different: Usually each plant has only one kind of flower. The female flowers would not be fertilized without the help of little insects called "fungus gnats," which carry the *pollen* from one plant to another.

Most arums live in the tropics, but a number are familiar wild plants in the United States and Canada. Skunk cabbage, green dragon, sweet flag, water arum, and arrow arum are common. They are all water-lovers: Jack-in-the-pulpit lives in damp woods and the others are plants of shorelines and wetlands. In tropical parts of the world, several species are grown for the thick starchy underground stems that are typical of arum plants. Taro is the most important of these food plants.

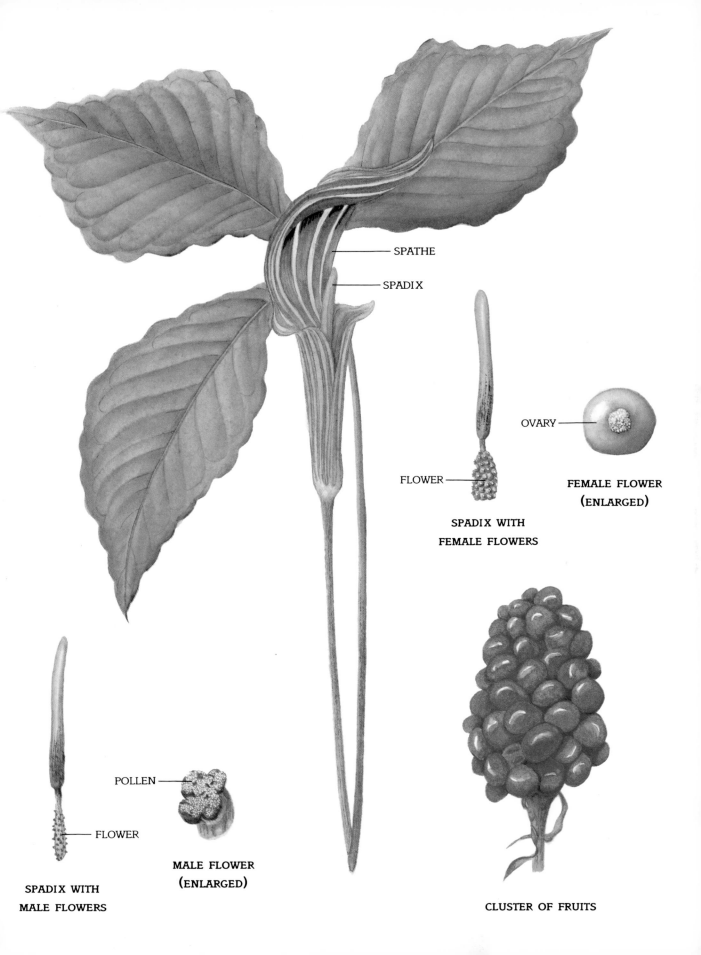

SPATHE

SPADIX

OVARY

**FEMALE FLOWER
(ENLARGED)**

FLOWER

**SPADIX WITH
FEMALE FLOWERS**

POLLEN

FLOWER

**MALE FLOWER
(ENLARGED)**

**SPADIX WITH
MALE FLOWERS**

CLUSTER OF FRUITS

Grass Family

GRAMINEAE
(gra-MIN-ee-ee)

Grass flowers are tiny and different from any other flowers in this book. They grow in a *spikelet* with a pair of little scales or *bracts* below it. Depending on the kind of grass, the spikelet may have one or more little flowers or florets. Most *florets* are only ⅛ to ¼ inch long.

Instead of sepals and petals, a grass floret is surrounded by a second pair of bracts. The male and female flower parts—usually three stamens and one pistil—are hidden inside these bracts until they are ready to bloom. The tip of the pistil, called the *stigma,* is usually split into two feathery branches. The fruit of a floret is a single grain.

Plants in the sedge family look like grasses and their flowers are similar. They can be told apart from grasses by looking at their stems. Grass stems are round and hollow, like very narrow drinking straws. However, when you cut through a sedge stem with a sharp knife, you see that it has a triangular shape and is usually filled with soft, spongy pith.

The florets on CRABGRASS grow on two to ten branches that attach at a single point on the top of the stem, similar to the fingers on a hand. It is a pest plant in our lawns and gardens; but wildlife eat the seeds, livestock graze on it, and in the southern United States, it is sometimes cut for hay.

The grass family is the single most important plant group for our food. It supplies all the grains—corn, wheat, rice, oats, barley, rye, and others. Some food sweeteners come from the family, too: Sugarcane and sorghum are grass plants.

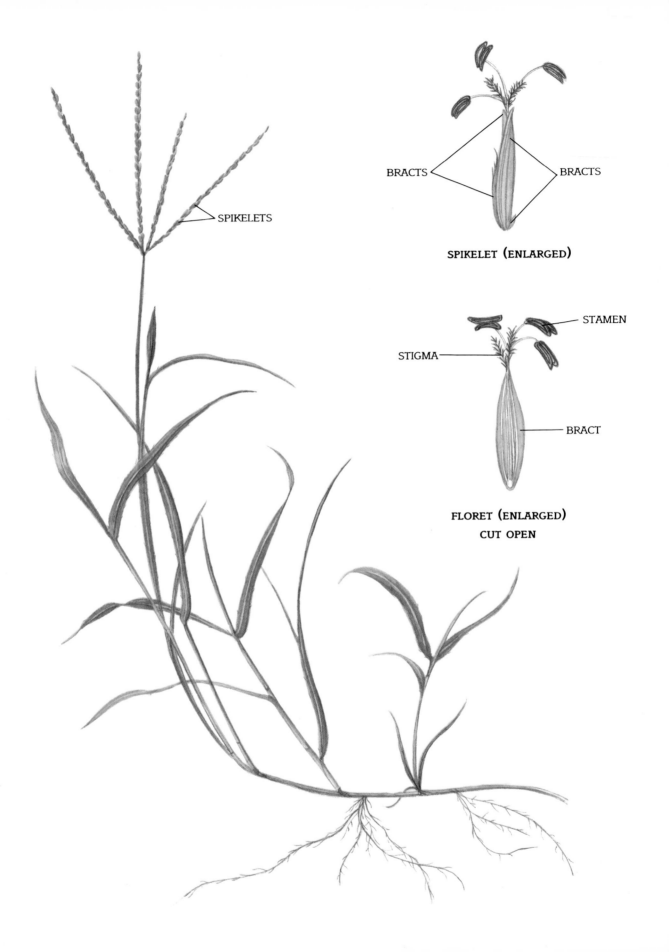

SPIKELETS

BRACTS

BRACTS

SPIKELET (ENLARGED)

STAMEN

STIGMA

BRACT

FLORET (ENLARGED)
CUT OPEN

Orchid Family

ORCHIDACEAE
(or-kid-DAY-see-ee)

We usually think of orchids as rare plants found only in the tropics. It's true that there are more orchids in tropical forests than anywhere else, but they also grow everywhere from Alaska and northern Sweden to the southern tip of South America and Africa. Some botanists say they are the largest of all the flowering plant families, with as many as 17,000 different kinds in the world. Over 150 species grow in the United States and Canada. Most of these have flowers that are smaller and less bright than the tropical orchids.

Like members of the lily family, an orchid has three sepals that may be just as colorful as the flower's three petals. The number of these parts is not always obvious, however. In some cases, two sepals—or even all three—are joined together. One of the three petals, called the "lip," is usually larger than the other petals and often different from them in shape and color. In many species, the big lip petal serves as a landing place for insects that pollinate the flower.

The most complicated part of an orchid flower is the arrangement of the male and female parts. The *style* and one or two stamens are joined into a single body called the *column,* which grows from the center of the flower. The *ovary* is below the flower. After the plant is fertilized, the ovary swells up and becomes a *capsule,* often filled with thousands of seeds as fine as dust. When it is ripe, the capsule splits open and the tiny seeds scatter in the wind.

LADY'S SLIPPERS (or moccasin flowers) are among our most beautiful native orchids. Eleven different species, with flowers of yellow, pink, or white, grow in North America. They take their name from the shape of the puffy lip petal. Two of their sepals are united into one and hang down behind the big lip. The column is hidden from sight by a winglike flap. Along with many of our other wild orchids, some species of lady's slippers are considered threatened plants in the United States and should never be picked.

Vanilla "beans"—the capsules of tropical vanilla vines—are grown for use as a food flavoring. Orchids are important in the florist trade, and many people enjoy the challenge of growing them as a hobby.

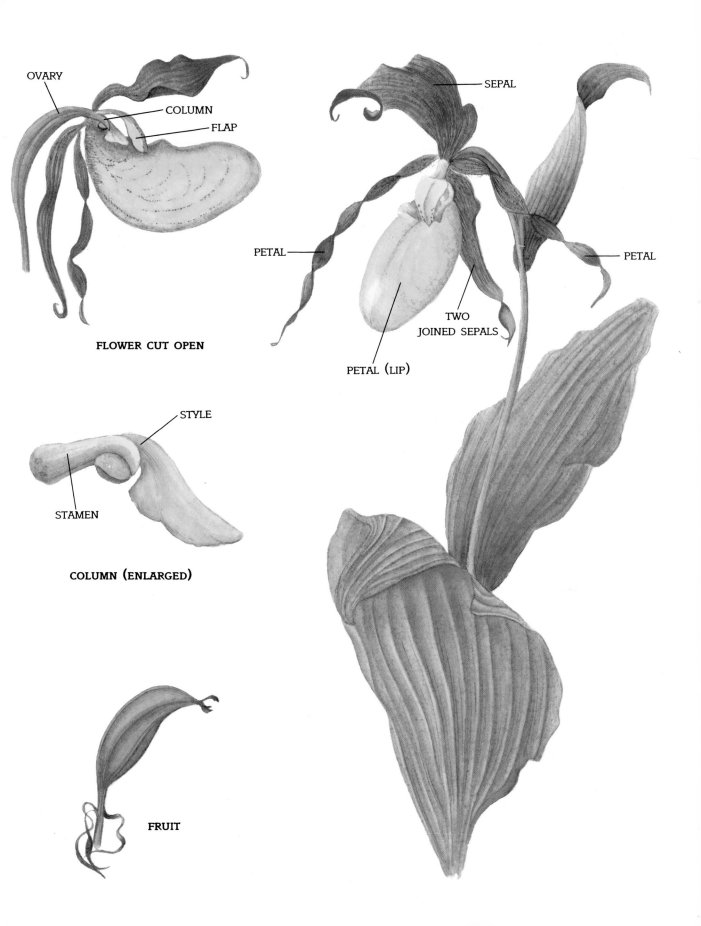

OVARY

COLUMN

FLAP

FLOWER CUT OPEN

SEPAL

PETAL

PETAL

TWO
JOINED SEPALS

PETAL (LIP)

STYLE

STAMEN

COLUMN (ENLARGED)

FRUIT

Glossary

berry—a fruit with soft, juicy pulp containing two or more seeds

bract—a special kind of leaf, usually growing just below the flower or the flower cluster

capsule—a dry fruit with two or more sections inside that splits open when it is ripe

column—the united stamens and style of an orchid flower

disk floret—a small tube-shaped flower on a composite plant

family—a group of genera that resemble each other

floral cup—a deep or shallow cup below the flower that has the sepals, petals, and stamens growing on its rim

floret—a very small flower. In the grasses, the bracts that surround the stamens and pistil are part of the floret.

fruit—a ripe ovary containing the seeds of a plant

genus (plural: *genera*)—a group of closely related plants or animals containing one or more different species

leaflet—one of the smaller leaf sections of a leaf that is divided into several separate parts

legume—a dry fruit of the pea family that usually splits open along two sides when it is ripe

nutlet—a small fruit with one seed inside and a hard covering

ovary—the bottom part of a pistil where the seeds grow

pappus—the bristles, scales, or hairs on top of the fruit of a composite plant

petal—the part of a flower that grows between the sepals and the stamens; usually the largest and brightest part of a flower

pistil—the female part of a flower

pod—a dry fruit (that is, one without pulp) with a number of seeds. Pods split open when they are ripe.

pollen—the small grains produced by stamens that fertilize an ovary

ray floret—a flattened, petal-like floret on a composite plant

receptacle—the top part of a stem where the flower parts are attached

sepal—the part of a flower that grows just outside the petals. Sepals cover the flower in bud.

simple (leaf)—all in one piece; not divided into separate sections

spadix—a thick spike covered by small flowers

spathe—a large bract attached below a flower cluster and often surrounding it

spikelet—a grass floret or cluster of florets, including the two small bracts that grow beneath it

stamen—the male part of a flower that produces pollen

stigma—the part of a pistil—usually at its top—where pollen must land before the flower can be fertilized

style—the part of a pistil that rises above the ovary

umbel—a cluster of flowers whose stalks all attach to the flower stem at one point